Beside the Seaside

in pictures

Edited by Helen J Bate

We're all going on a summer holiday!

Photographs: Two young girls holding dolls and a bucket and spade lean out of a railway carriage window as they depart for their summer holiday from Euston Station, London. Fred Morley / Hulton Archive / Getty Images

Quotation from song Summer Holiday sung by Cliff Richard.

Where did you get that hat?

Painting: Along the Shore, 1914 (tempera on silk) by Joseph Edward Southall
(1861-1944) Reproduced with permission of the Barrow Family.
Oldham Gallery, UK / The Bridgeman Art Library

Where Did You Get That Hat - from a Broadside Ballad written around 1880-1900

enjoying the view

from the giant wheel

on the Palace Pier, Brighton.

Photograph: David Savill/Hulton Archive/Getty Images

Patience

is the best remedy
for every trouble.

Painting: Studies of Animals (S.Ex.2-1885) by Stephen Briggs Carlil (fl.1888-1903)

Quotation: Titus Maccius Plautus 254BC-184BC

All animals, except man,

know that the principal business of life is to enjoy it.

I must go down to the sea again,

to the lonely seas and the sky,

All I ask is a tall ship

and a star to steer her by.

Quotation: From Sea Fever by John Masefield (1878-1967) by permission of
The Society of Authors as the Literary Representative of the Estate of John Masefield

Photographs: A group of children trying to refloat the coaster 'Penton' which drifted on
to Gorleston beach in Norfolk during gales. Fred Morley / Hulton Archive / Getty Images

I regard golf

as an expensive way of playing marbles.

William Banks Fortescue

who painted this picture, studied art in
Paris and in Venice. He arrived in
Newlyn, Cornwall in 1885 and became
a well-known figure in the local villages
riding about on a grey horse, with his
easel strapped to his back.

Painting: The Fish Fag by William Banks Fortescue (1855-1924)
Atkinson Art Gallery, Southport, Lancashire, UK. The Bridgeman Art Library/Getty Images

There are two things to aim at in life:

first, to get what you want; and after that, to enjoy it.

Photograph: Boy eating ice cream © Graham Franks/FoodAndDrink

Quotation: Logan Pearsall Smith, Afterthoughts, 1931

Mud
Flats

A worker involved in the scheme to reclaim land from the sea for agriculture, leaves footprints in the mud.

She sells seashells
On the seashore

You are my
sunshine

Painting: La Plage 1900
by Alfred Victor Fournier (1872-1924)
Fine Art Photographic/Getty Images

Quotation from song
'You are my sunshine'
by Jimmy Davis & Charles Mitchell

Better to get up late and be

wide awake,

than to get up early and be

asleep all day.

Main photograph: A young competitor at the Southend Fishing Festival. E Dean/Hulton Archive/Getty Images

26 Quotation: Anonymous

Brighton West Pier

was built in 1866 using dozens of cast iron columns screwed into the seabed. A part of the pier collapsed in a storm in December 2002. In March and May 2003, arson attacks destroyed much of the remainder.

Painting: Brighton West Pier, 2004 (oil on canvas), Tom Young (Contemporary Artist)/Private Collection/The Bridgeman Art Library

Of all the things you wear,

your expression is
the most important.

Photographs: Fisherman with lobster catch ©Nick Smith/FoodAndDrink

Quotation: Janet Lane

There is no such thing

in anyone's life as an unimportant day.

Painting: 'Whitley Bay' by F Donald Blake (1908-1997) detail from
British Rail poster, 1951. Science & Society Picture Library
Quotation: Alexander Woollcott (American author)

Once you have travelled,

the voyage never ends,
but is played out
over and over again
in the quietest chambers...

Photograph: Three young boys sailing a home-made raft at Frinton-on-Sea, Essex, by Reg Speller/Hulton Archive/Getty Images
Quotation from The Prince of Tides by Pat Conroy (US novelist)

Things can look dark, then a break shows in the clouds,

and all is changed.

Photograph: Seamill, North Ayrshire, Scotland, with the Isle of Arran in the background by James H Willetts

Quotation: E. B. White
US author & humorist (1899-1985)

I do like to be beside the seaside,

Oh I do like to be beside the sea!
I do like to stroll along the
prom, prom, prom,
Where the brass band plays

Tiddleyompompom!

Words from song 'I do Like to be Beside the Seaside' by John A Glover-Kind

My soul is awakened,

my spirit is soaring
And carried aloft on the wings of the breeze;
For above and around me
the wild wind is roaring,
Arousing to rapture the earth and the seas.

Painting: Rain squall over Covesea Skerries Lighthouse by Jolomo
(John Lowrie Morrison) one of Scotland's best loved contemporary artists.
This painting is reproduced here by kind permission of Mr Morrison.

Quotation: 'Lines composed in a wood on a windy day' by Anne Bronte (1820-49)

Cockles

are a popular type of
edible shellfish. They are still
collected by raking them from
the sands at low tide.

Main photograph: Cockle gatherers at Pendawdd, South Wales.
Fox Photo's/Hulton Archive/Getty Images

The end
of a long day

46

Photograph: Six girls, chosen by Picture Post to visit popular seaside resorts as a part of a holiday game with a cash prize, look out to sea from Eastbourne Pier.

Left to right; Jean Martin, Mavis Bute, Frances Hamill, Anne West, Rita Orme and Anne Miller. Carl Sutton / Hulton Archive / Getty Images

**Pictures
to share**

Acknowledgements
Our thanks to the many contributors who have allowed their
text or imagery to be used for a reduced or no fee.
Thanks also to all those who assisted in the development of this
book by helping with or taking part in trials.

All effort has been made to contact copyright holders.
If you own the copyright for work that is represented, but have
not been contacted, please get in touch via our website.

Thanks to our sponsors

ANDREWS CHARITABLE TRUST

Some quotations have been provided by
'Chambers Dictionary of Quotations',
Chambers Harrap Publishers Ltd, 2005
Others have been provided by www.quotationspage.com and
www.quotegarden.com

Published by
Pictures to Share Community Interest Company.
Peckforton, Cheshire
www.picturestoshare.co.uk

Printed in England by
Burlington Press, Station Road, Foxton
Cambridgeshire CB22 6SA